MY BODY Inside and Out!

What Happens When I Sleep?

by Ruth Owen

Consultant:

Suzy Gazlay, MA
Recipient, Presidential Award for Excellence in Science Teaching

Ruby Tuesday Books

Published in 2014 by Ruby Tuesday Books Ltd.

Editor: Mark J. Sachner
Designers: Tammy West and Emma Randall

Photo credits:
Science Photo Library: 19 (bottom); Shutterstock:
Cover, 1, 4–5, 7, 8–9, 12–13, 14–15, 17, 18, 19 (top), 20, 23;
Superstock: 11, 21.

Library of Congress Control Number: 2013908618

ISBN 978-1-909673-30-4

Printed and published in the United States of America

For further information including rights and permissions
requests, please contact our Customer Service Department
at 877-337-8577.

Contents

Words shown in **bold** in the text are
explained in the glossary.

Time to Sleep

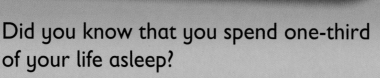

Did you know that you spend one-third of your life asleep?

That probably sounds like a big waste of time, but sleep is very important for your body.

It might seem as if your body shuts down when you go to sleep.

In fact, it is busy all night making repairs, helping you grow, and getting you ready for a new day. Let's check it out.

What happens when I sleep?

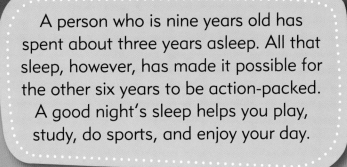

A person who is nine years old has spent about three years asleep. All that sleep, however, has made it possible for the other six years to be action-packed. A good night's sleep helps you play, study, do sports, and enjoy your day.

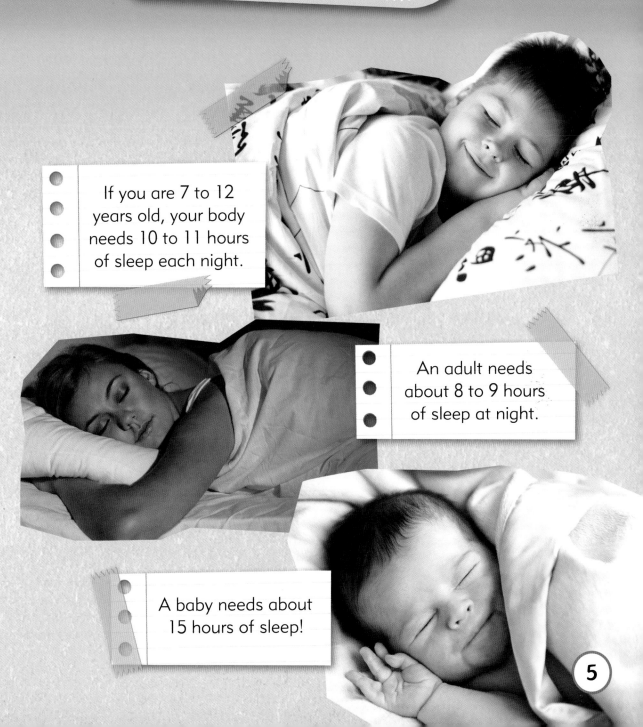

If you are 7 to 12 years old, your body needs 10 to 11 hours of sleep each night.

An adult needs about 8 to 9 hours of sleep at night.

A baby needs about 15 hours of sleep!

Your Body Clock
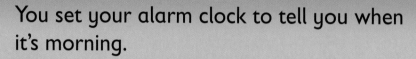

You set your alarm clock to tell you when it's morning.

Your body actually has its own clock inside, however.

Your body clock is a part of your **brain** that **detects** sunlight and darkness.

As night falls, your brain detects the darkness and starts making a chemical called **melatonin**.

This chemical gets you ready for bed by making you feel sleepy.

In the morning, your body clock detects sunlight and knows it's time for you to wake up.

Having a bright light near your bed, such as a computer or TV screen, can make it hard to fall asleep. That's because the light makes your body clock think that it must be daytime!

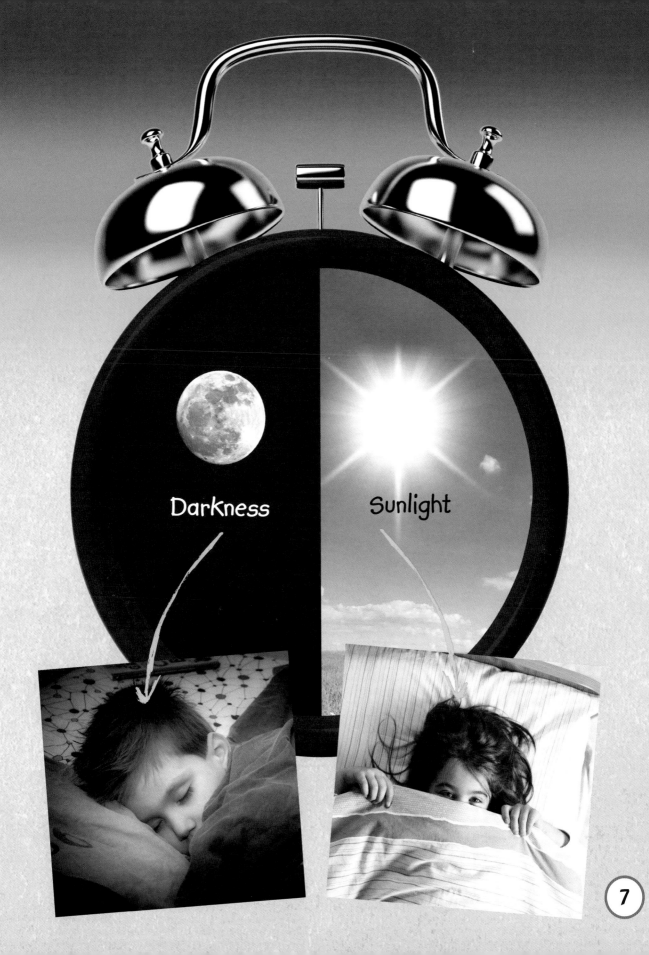

Darkness

Sunlight

Your Sleep Cycle

It might feel as if all sleep is the same, but it's not.

Your sleep goes through a cycle, or pattern, that has five stages.

Stage 1 is when you are just dozing off and you are half awake and half asleep.

Next, your body goes into stage 2, and you actually fall asleep.

During stages 3 and 4, you are sleeping deeply.

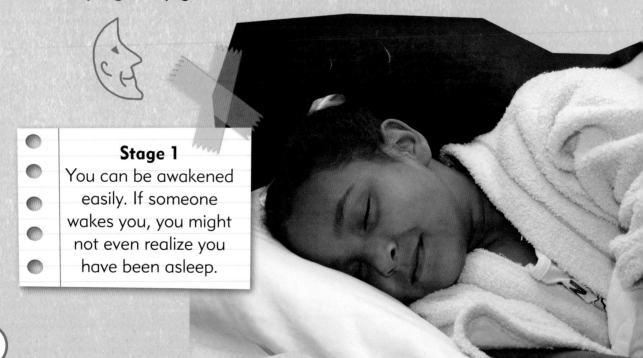

Stage 1
You can be awakened easily. If someone wakes you, you might not even realize you have been asleep.

8

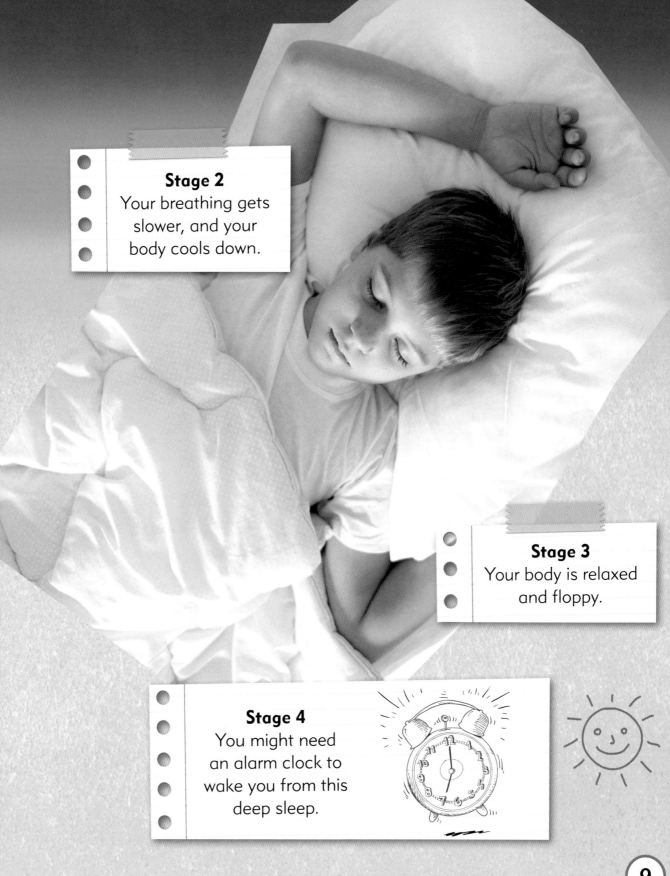

Stage 2
Your breathing gets slower, and your body cools down.

Stage 3
Your body is relaxed and floppy.

Stage 4
You might need an alarm clock to wake you from this deep sleep.

REM Sleep

The fifth and final stage in your sleep cycle is known as **REM sleep**.

REM stands for "rapid eye movement" sleep.

When you are having REM sleep, your eyes move about rapidly, or quickly.

If you watch people who are in this sleep stage, you may see their eyelids flickering.

During REM sleep you have **dreams**, and your brain is nearly as busy as it is during daytime.

During REM sleep, your body barely moves. Scientists think your brain might switch off your body's movements. This keeps your body still and stops it from acting out your dreams!

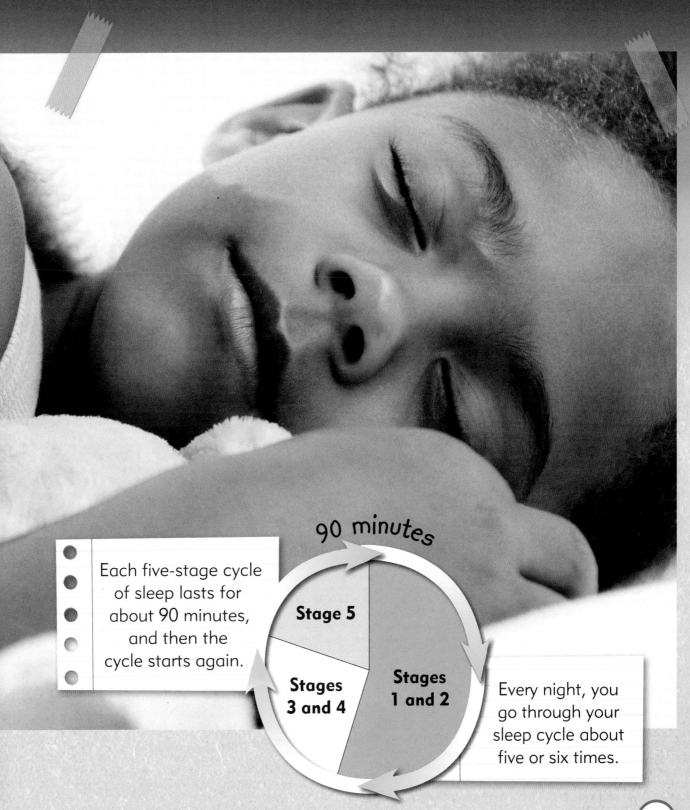

Each five-stage cycle of sleep lasts for about 90 minutes, and then the cycle starts again.

90 minutes

Stage 5

Stages 3 and 4

Stages 1 and 2

Every night, you go through your sleep cycle about five or six times.

Why Do We Dream?

During your times of REM sleep, you have dreams.

Each night, you have at least four or five dreams, but you don't always remember them.

That's because you usually only remember dreams that happen just before you wake up.

Scientists have been studying people's dreams for years, but they still don't know why we dream.

One idea is that while you are asleep, your brain is sorting things out.

As your brain organizes all your thoughts and memories from your day, it creates dreams.

In a dream, you might fly like a bird or get chased by dinosaurs. No matter how weird your dream is, your brain makes it feel very real. Dreams aren't real, though, and dreaming something doesn't mean it will happen!

A dream can feel as if
it's lasted for hours,
but most dreams only
last for a few minutes.

13

Sleep for Your Brain

You might be asleep, but your brain is still busy all night.

No one knows for sure what our brains do at night, but scientists have lots of ideas.

They think that as we sleep, our brains sort and store information from our day.

Our amazing brains might also be fixing parts of themselves that we use for thinking and learning things.

What scientists do know for sure is that sleep helps our brains work better.

zzZZzz

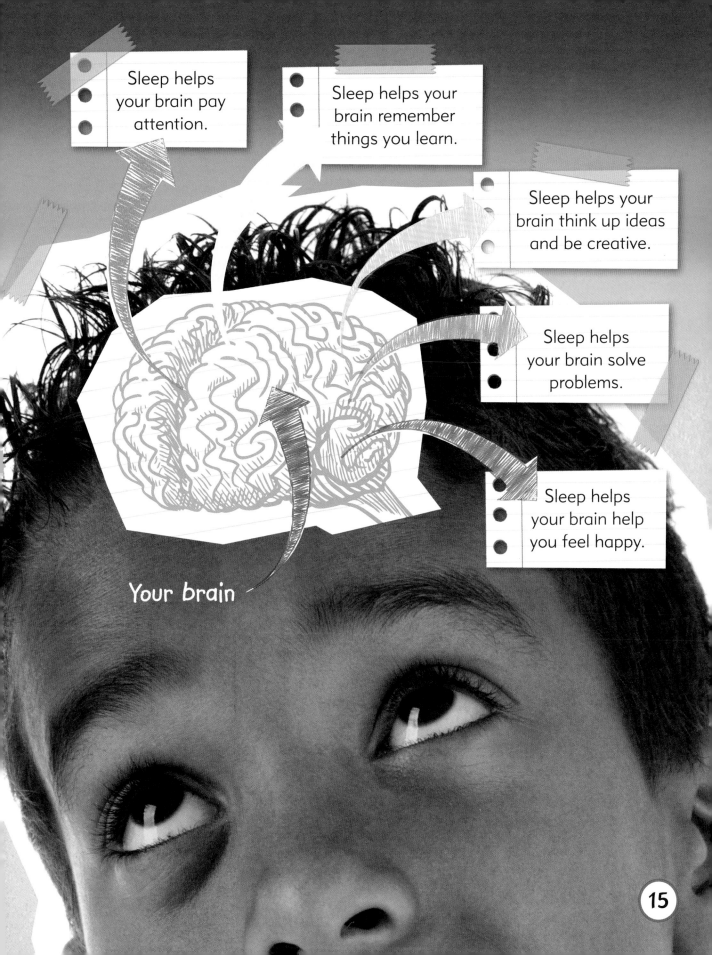

Sleep for Your Heart

Your **heart** is just one of hundreds of **muscles** in your body.

All day and all night, your heart is **pumping** your **blood** around your body.

During the day, your heart beats, and pumps, about 70 times each minute.

When you are asleep, your heart gets to slow down a little and beat fewer times.

This means sleeping gives your heart a rest and helps keep it healthy.

From blinking to kicking a ball, your muscles are hard at work all day. While you sleep, your muscles get a chance to rest.

Your blood has many important jobs to do. For example, it carries **oxygen** around your body and delivers **nutrients** for energy.

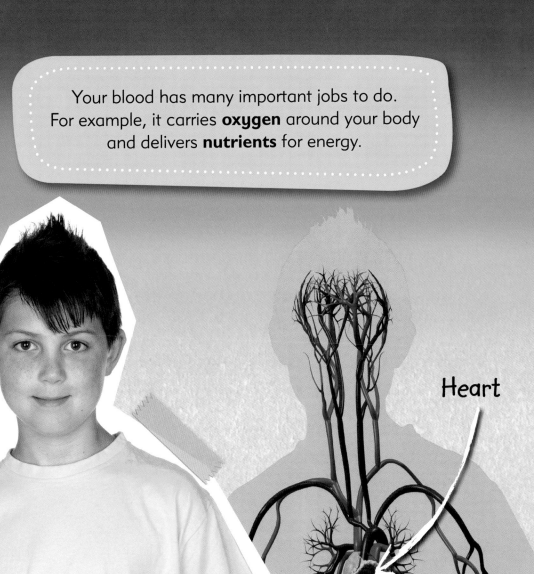

Heart

The blue and red tubes in this picture are veins and arteries that carry blood around your body.

Sleep for Fixing and Growing

When you are awake, your body's energy is used for studying, talking, and playing.

When you are asleep, your body can use its energy to make repairs.

For example, your skin grows faster as you sleep to heal cuts and scrapes.

As you sleep, your body also uses its energy to make your bones, muscles, and other body parts grow.

You won't notice it's happened, but in the morning, you will be just a teeny, tiny bit taller!

While you are sleeping, your body produces chemicals that it uses to fight off illnesses.

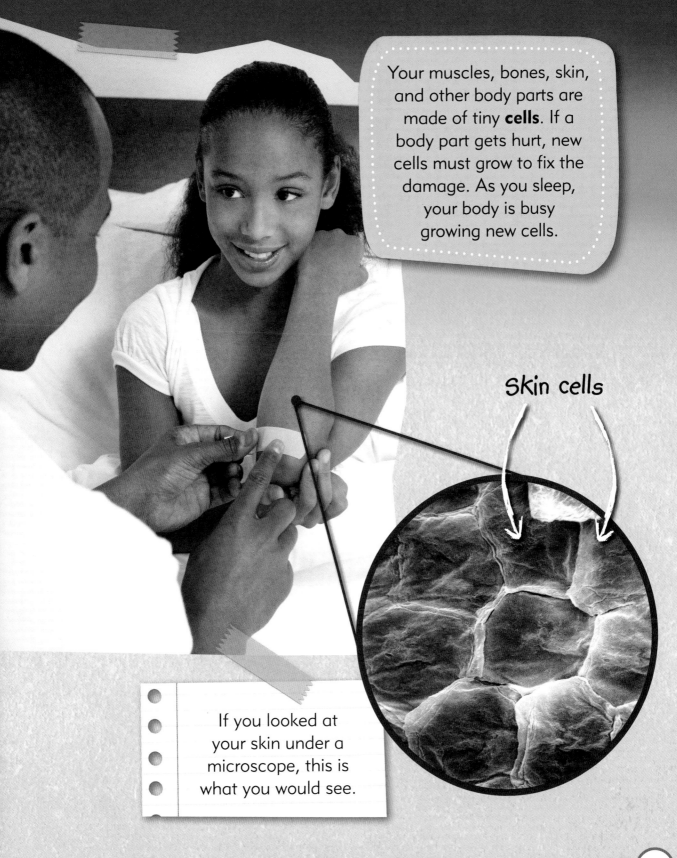

Your muscles, bones, skin, and other body parts are made of tiny **cells**. If a body part gets hurt, new cells must grow to fix the damage. As you sleep, your body is busy growing new cells.

Skin cells

If you looked at your skin under a microscope, this is what you would see.

Sleep = More Fun

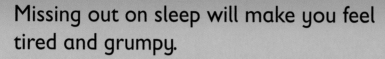

Missing out on sleep will make you feel tired and grumpy.

Your schoolwork may seem more difficult, and you might forget what you have learned.

Games and sports won't be as much fun, because you will have less energy.

It might seem like going to bed is a big waste of time, but it's not.

When you get plenty of sleep, you're happier, healthier, and ready to have fun!

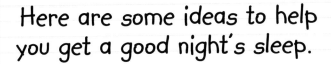

Here are some ideas to help you get a good night's sleep.

Try to go to bed at the same time each night. Your body will get used to the routine, and it will know it's time to sleep.

Make sure your bedroom is quiet and dark.

Don't watch TV or play games in bed. Make your bed a place for sleeping.

Glossary

blood (BLUHD) The red liquid that carries oxygen and nutrients to cells in every part of your body.

brain (BRANE) The body part that controls your senses, thinking, and movements. Messages between your brain and other parts of your body are sent and received through cells called nerves.

cells (SELZ) Very tiny parts of a living thing. Your bones, muscles, skin, hair, and every part of you are made of cells.

detect (dee-TECT) To recognize or identify something.

dream (DREEM) A series of thoughts, images, and feelings that take place in your mind while you are asleep.

heart (HART) The large, muscular organ, or body part, in your chest that pumps blood throughout your body.

melatonin (mel-uh-TOH-nin) A chemical made by the body that helps control your daily cycle, or pattern, of sleeping and waking.

muscle (MUH-suhl) A part of the body that contracts, or tightens up, and relaxes to produce movement. Muscles use energy that comes from food.

nutrient (NOO-tree-uhnt) A substance taken in by the body, usually through food, that the body needs to grow, get energy, and stay healthy.

oxygen (OX-ih-jin) An invisible gas in the air that living things need to breathe.

pump (PUHMP) To force or push something so it moves in one direction, as if driven by a machine.

REM sleep (REM SLEEP) A period of sleep that happens several times during a night's sleep. REM stands for "rapid eye movement." During this time, the brain is very active, and you have dreams.

Index

Read More

Culbert, Timothy, and Rebecca Kajander. *Be the Boss of Your Sleep: Self-Care for Kids (Be the Boss of Your Body).* Minneapolis: Free Spirit Publishing (2007).

Huebner, Dawn. *What to Do When You Dread Your Bed: A Kid's Guide to Overcoming Problems With Sleep (What to Do Guides for Kids).* Washington, DC: Magination Press (2008).

Learn More Online

To learn more about what happens when you sleep, go to
www.rubytuesdaybooks.com/mybodysleep